POETRY TOMES

VOICES OF THE FUTURE

EDITED BY SARAH WATERHOUSE

First published in Great Britain in 2023 by:

YoungWriters®
Est. 1991

Young Writers
Remus House
Coltsfoot Drive
Peterborough
PE2 9BF
Telephone: 01733 890066
Website: www.youngwriters.co.uk

All Rights Reserved
Book Design by Ashley Janson
© Copyright Contributors 2023
Softback ISBN 978-1-80459-774-3

Printed and bound in the UK by BookPrintingUK
Website: www.bookprintinguk.com
YB0556F

FOREWORD

For Young Writers' latest competition we invited primary school pupils to enroll at a new school, Poetry Towers, where they could let their imaginations roam free.

At Poetry Towers the timetable of subjects on offer is unlimited, so pupils could choose any topic that inspired them and write in any poetry style. We provided free resources including lesson plans, poetry guides and inspiration and examples to help pupils craft a piece of writing they can be proud of.

Here at Young Writers our aim is to encourage creativity in children and to inspire a love of the written word, so it's great to get such an amazing response, with some absolutely fantastic poems. It's important for children to express themselves and a great way to engage them is to allow them to write about what they care about. The result is a varied collection of poems with a range of styles and techniques that showcase their creativity and writing ability.

We'd like to congratulate all the young poets in this anthology, the latest alumni of the Young Writers' academy of poetry and rhyme. We hope this inspires them to continue with their creative writing.

CONTENTS

Edward Wilson Primary School, Westminster

Yasmin Saemh (7)	1

Longfield Primary School, Harrow

Emma Jayakumar (10)	2
Aashish Gupta (10)	4
Amber Alam (10)	6
Mia Padhlar (10)	7
Ram Anand Kesar (9)	8
Khushi Rashmi Darbar (9)	9
Helena Hope (10)	10
Swagatha Paranthaman (10)	11
Ishaani Mistry (10)	12
Akshara Krishna (10)	13
Krishaa Kanodia (10)	14
Hetakshi Patel (10)	15
Serena Valand (10)	16
Aaryan Chudasama (9)	17
Saara Ahmed (9)	18
Yug Ruparelia (10)	19
Zoya Naqshbandi (10)	20
Roberta Ion (9)	21
Jodele Foster-Wickham (10)	22
Shiven Joshi (10)	23
Inayah Khan (10)	24
Shlok Patel (10)	25
Kairos Sunuwar (9)	26
Jasmin Sehdev (10)	27
Vibha Vikrenth (10)	28
Hrishi Patel (10)	29
Maryam Mafaz (9)	30
Selina Parekh (10)	31

St James' CE Primary School, Ashton-Under-Lyne

Merwa Khayyam (8)	32
Luca Oncica (8)	34
Rayaan Ashraf (8)	36
Maddison Cook (9)	37
Jayden Verdes (9)	38
Confidence Igwe (9)	39
Abdul Cande (8)	40
Ume Noreen (9)	41
Ismail Raza (8)	42
Hannah Moyhuddin (9)	43
Zainab Ehsan (9)	44
Olivia Kenyon (9)	45
Ziad Bowden (9)	46
Oscar Carr (9)	47
Ubaid Mirza (9)	48
Imaan Shahzad (9)	49
Awaais Rashid (8)	50
Haleema Mahmood (9)	51
Lana Jamal (9)	52
Ismail Mohammed (9)	53
Zara Vaughan (8)	54
Roman Ramezan (9)	55
Freddie Peaterson (9)	56

St Mary Redcliffe CE Primary School, Windmill Hill

Myra Lepcha Shaw (9)	57
Isobel Brown (9)	58
Jonah Smith (8) & Juliet Croft (8)	60
Evie Rose Henry (11)	62
Sasha Penman (11)	64

Scarlet Porter (11), Megan Harvey (11) & Megan Anthony (11)	65
Amelie Williams (11) & Audrey Gibbard (11)	66
Emilia Turner (9) & Shameika Sappleton (9)	67
Salwa Caraye (10), Hamda & Scarlet Porter (11)	68
Clio Mongon (9)	69
Maisey-Jade Arthur Brooks (11)	70
Amelie Williams (11)	71
Minna Kauntze (9)	72
Evan Cormack (9)	73
Ta'Shiyah Douglas (9)	74
Maggie Wilshire & Iona Miller (11)	75
Caolan (10)	76
Barnaby Watson (8)	77
Stella Simson (8)	78
Juliet Croft (8)	79
Megan Anthony (11)	80
Anya Clements (7)	81
Ophelia Bell (11)	82
Stevie Rogers (8)	83
Isaac Couzens (10)	84
Sebastian Flower (11)	85
Veda (9)	86

Stalham Academy, Stalham

Sarah Pegg (10)	87
Tommy Austrin (9)	88
Max Tansley (9)	89
Lily Terrington (10)	90
Ally Mcclenaghan (9)	91
Maddie Fisher (10)	92
Florence Perrins (9)	93
Kaiden Chippindale (9)	94
Matilda Addy (10)	95
Ruby Hughes (10)	96
Harvey Mackin (9)	97
Finlay Whittaker-Benson (10)	98
Erin Woolston (10)	99

Jimmy Thrower (9)	100
Archie Coman (9)	101
Amelia Hudson (10)	102
Isabella Fox (9)	103
Thomas Jackson (10)	104
Corey Taylor (10)	105
Freya Cooper (9)	106
Shayla Jarmey (9)	107
George Grady (10)	108
Harry Hyde (10)	109
Emmerson Frost (10)	110
Isabella Cossey (10)	111
Wilbur Dodd (9)	112
Amy Fearn (10)	113
Megan Mace (10)	114
Logan Wood (10)	115
Tyler Clarke (10)	116
Brooke Beales (9)	117
Olive Nichols (10)	118
Sophia Bell (9)	119
Mia Eglington (10)	120
Archie Harvey (10)	121
Hazel Smith (9)	122
Jessica Sharp (10)	123
Charlie-Jordan Beales (10)	124
Benjamin Hobbs (9)	125
Jessie Vaughan (10)	126

Tregadillett Primary School, Tregadillett

Lyndsey Bourne (10)	127
Julia Kaletha (9)	128
Lena Pidgeon (9)	129
Evie Massey (10)	130
Jason Langdale (9)	131

Walmley Junior School, Sutton Coldfield

Elodie Harding (10)	132
Isabella Jagroo (9)	134
Cindy Ding (9)	136
Elora Sallis (8) & Tilly Soesan (9)	138

Pihu Bhalla (7)	139
Eloise George (9) & Talia Matar (9)	140
Poppy Bowen (7)	141
Eva Beauchamp (9)	142
Edith Drysdale (8)	143
Anneisea Thoto Cameron (10)	144
Veer Bhalla (10)	145
Tabitha Abraham (8)	146
Raine Dee (8)	147
Daisy Bray (9)	148
Erynn Jacks (8)	149
Amy Kong (9)	150
Gianna Antonia Jeevan (11)	151
Rehan Afzal (9)	152
Oliver Mushing (8)	153
Maisy Coombs (11)	154
Imogen Holliday (9)	155
Daya Chana (10)	156
Lily Miller (11)	157
Reggie Butler (9)	158
Gracelyn Noby (8)	159
Leah Sangster (9)	160
Zaynab Deen (9)	161
Mia-Rose Burbidge (8)	162
Elise Lee Allen (9)	163
Alex Husak (8)	164
Ayla Noor Bajwa (7)	165

Westcott Primary School, Hull

Erijesu Adeniran (10)	166
Phoebe McCoid (10)	167
Eva Brewin (10)	168
Lily Procter (10)	169
Savannah Booker (9)	170
Evie Wharam (9)	171
Mia Hampshire (10)	172
Elise Hampshire (10)	173
Isabelle Kirby (9)	174
Neve Symons (9)	175
Gracie Reid (10)	176
Emily Underwood (10)	177
Ebony Barker (10)	178

Jessica Atkin (10)	179
Charlie Davison (10)	180
Ellis Hall (10)	181
Phoebe Fletcher (9)	182
Marjan Khaksar (10)	183
Jessica Todd (10)	184
Layla Carr (9)	185
Mila Fleming (10)	186
Evie Sellers (9)	187
Maria Ciuperca (10)	188
Noah Sanderson (10)	189
Elsie Mae Cassells Robinson (9)	190
Joey Dale (10)	191
Alfie Cawkell (10)	192
Olivia Hickson (10)	193
Jasmine Thompson (10)	194
Deacon Russell (10)	195
Oliver Anderson (10)	196
James Cooper (10)	197
Oliver Priest (9)	198
Archie W (9)	199

THE POEMS

Monkey Meal

In the forest, in the tree,
There is a monkey swinging fast and free,
Hanging by his hand and feet,
He looks, you see a delicious treat
Ripe bananas everywhere
Which juicy one should he get?
Monkey grabs
Monkey cheers
Monkey peels
Monkey got his monkey meal!

Yasmin Saemh (7)
Edward Wilson Primary School, Westminster

Where Adventures Can Take You!

Adventures can take you anywhere.
You go by train and stay on the train
Don't even know where that train might be taking you
And we call that an adventure!
Exciting, extreme, exotic adventures will lead you to becoming a champion.
You don't know what to do one day
And my words are 'never let your fears control you ever in your life!'
So, you should cover the Earth before it covers you.
You know you can do this,
So, you should be mustering your courage.

Your mind is the one taking you to these places.
I am the one saying to go on that adventure that you have in your mind now
And just roll with it.
Keep going, don't stop.
If you stop, your dream will end

And bear in mind that I want you to be able to achieve this dream that you have.
This is my dream,
I want you to be able to do this.
Because, inside, deep down
I know that you can do this
You will also feel proud of yourself and that moment really feels good
Because you can feel it as well as me.
So, we all know that this is you going on that big adventure!
Be brave, fearless, wondrous, happy,
Adventurous when it comes to an adventure!

Emma Jayakumar (10)
Longfield Primary School, Harrow

A Dream

A dream is what you implore
And what heights your curiosity can reach
A dream is the acquaintance of your hope
And what your creativity can achieve

Dreams are the branches of a puzzle
A puzzle that cannot be solved
They are your only hope
Of a future you believe in

A dream is an emotion
An emotion you treasure
A dream is your future
Full of comfort and happiness

Just what I said is not quite right
It's not just a random puzzle
Or your only hope
It's truly your imagination

I do really assure you
With my full consent
Your unique dream
Will definitely come true

So, next time you dream
Close your eyes in the depth of your soul
And focus...
On your wonderful dream.

Aashish Gupta (10)
Longfield Primary School, Harrow

Candy Land

A place full of sugar canes and sweets,
Chocolate crispies and sherbert treats,
Candy Land is a child's happy place,
Oh, if you could see the cheerfulness and joy on their faces,
A land full of candyfloss clouds and jelly-bean seas,
Haribo flowers and sugar plum trees
Delicious varieties of doughnuts and cake,
Literally, all the yum-yums you could bake.
Mountains of fudge and valleys of toffee
Marshes of tiramisu that just tastes like coffee,
Gingerbread houses with gingerbread men,
Chocolate eggs laid by chocolate hen,
Lakes of melted chocolate and volcanoes of popping candy,
This world of sweets seems to be so happy and dandy,
But here is one last secret about this sugary nation,
It only exists in your deepest imagination!

Amber Alam (10)
Longfield Primary School, Harrow

Living Nature

In the field where I had my picnic,
I saw a ruby-red rose
Which stood in a particular pose,
The thorns were a light lime-green colour,
And were as sharp as a long spiky blade,
Which somehow made me afraid.

Swoosh, whoosh! The leaves started to rumble
Just as the hungry wolf's belly started to grumble,
The grass started to whoosh
Right after, the wind started to push
As if it was angry.
I started to watch the tulips grow,
Which took time and effort, so it was going quite slow.

The old tree started to wrinkle,
Just as the leaves started to shrink,
Watching all the bugs crawl around,
Made a peculiar sound.

Mia Padhlar (10)
Longfield Primary School, Harrow

My Life In The Trenches: The Storm

Day after day, I painstakingly wake up with empty beds of brave soldiers,
Vast deafening shells land with a hint of sorrow,
I curiously wonder how many more battles I'll survive,
The storm approaches.

As brave as Napolean, I keep my stand against the storm,
Every day, my heart courageously states: "Never give up hope, for this is your country."
Even if we're outnumbered, we shan't run like cowards,
Even if we fall back into darkness again,
We'll never give up hope.

My duty savagely calls,
Boom! In my last breaths,
I ponder on my sacrifice, my nation,
I die with pride from serving my motherland.

Ram Anand Kesar (9)
Longfield Primary School, Harrow

Nature's Life

The aroma of fresh air rejuvenated me,
The flowers were beautiful, a vibrant sea
The melodious birdsong which my heart danced to.
An encouraging harmony which will enchant you.

Rays of light pirouetted onto verdant meadows
That are full of sunlight's yellow,
Vegetation encircling formidable mountains
While icy waters form fountains.

The lustrous petals on my fingers
And the tickling sensation lingers
The tree and its auburn coat
Listen to the *honk* of the sea's boat.

So now, when the sun goes down,
A new dawn is found,
And so, when the sun goes up,
We will give it all our tuck.

Khushi Rashmi Darbar (9)
Longfield Primary School, Harrow

The Wonderful Countryside

The countryside is a natural wonder,
With surprises, maybe just over yonder,
It's a great place for both young and old,
There's always something to do, truth be told!

The clouds are dancing across the sky,
Lie down on a hill and watch them float by,
While sheep calmly just graze just o'er the hills,
The mesmerising sunset is something that thrills.

Sleep in a cottage and warm fires will,
Slowly guide you to bed, there's no need to be chilled,
As your head meets the pillow, you quietly say,
"I'll enjoy the countryside for another day."

Helena Hope (10)
Longfield Primary School, Harrow

Seasons Of Nature!

Spring is when daffodils glow,
Spring is the time where gardens grow
Summer, summer
I'm so glad you're here
Summer, summer
Let's give it a cheer
Summer, summer
I'll meet you at the park!
Till it gets dark
How silently they tumble down
And come to a rest upon the ground
To lay the carpet rich and rare
Beneath the trees, without a care
'Oh, the weather outside is frightful
But the fire is so delightful
And since we've no place to go
Let it snow! Let it snow! Let it snow!'

Swagatha Paranthaman (10)
Longfield Primary School, Harrow

The Iron Man

His arms came out of the grassy hills,
Everyone was frightened with cold, hard chills.
Heavy arms and metal hands,
The Iron Man ruined all the lands.

Crash! Boom! Bang!
The Iron Man sprang.
Clink! Clonk! Clash!
The Iron Man's arms came out like a flash.

Babies crying as loud as a roar,
The adults felt like they were in war
Until the farmers and villagers heard,
They thought it was very absurd...

Iron Man, Iron Man, go away,
Iron Man, Iron Man, don't come back,
Iron Man, Iron Man, we will attack!

Ishaani Mistry (10)
Longfield Primary School, Harrow

I Hate Literary Devices

I hate similes,
As they are like rampaging monsters,
With hearts as cold as ice,
Trying to get me.

I hate metaphors,
As they are gloomy lights,
On a pitch-black countryside night.

I hate personification,
Because it is a sinister laugh,
Slicing me in half.

I hate onomatopoeia,
It hits me with a *bang!*
I'm not the best at bright ideas,
So, like cymbals, it goes *clang!*

I hate literary devices
I want to shut them up
In a bowl or cup.
My advice is to give up!

Akshara Krishna (10)
Longfield Primary School, Harrow

Open Your Eyes

We need to be sustainable,
So our future will be attainable.
We need to open our eyes and stop being blind,
Let's leave all our mistakes behind.
Stop our selfishness,
And to Mother Nature let us give kindness.
Animals are dying,
Mother Nature is crying.
Listen to her pleads,
And start planting seeds.
In the oceans, plastic say,
"God will make us pay."
God has gifted us with glory,
Don't make *that* his story.
Where are all the trees?
Oh, please, give Earth some peace.

Krishaa Kanodia (10)
Longfield Primary School, Harrow

Mother Earth

Each act of compassion,
For dear *Mother Earth*,
What a great place to be found,
A home planet for you and me,
But now *Mother Earth* is crying.

So, pick up your garbage,
Don't leave it for me,
I'll be doing my own part,
Which is planting a tree,
You will understand its worth.

Yet no one understands *your* worth,
People are destroying you, due to their greed,
We have to take action now,
It's all up to us,
To save our dear *Mother Earth*.

Hetakshi Patel (10)
Longfield Primary School, Harrow

Bingo The Flamingo

Did you hear about the flamingo called Bingo?
She won every fun game,
Her head was full of strategies and ways to think,
That she needed an extra brain!

She was the best at
Noughts and crosses, and chess.
She has a lot of fun
All thanks to her very lucky dress!

Miss Bingo the flamingo
Did not even try to win,
Her lucky dress was a robot
And it threw her in the bin!

Bingo the flamingo was a winner no more
Her betrayer of a dress shunned her behind the door!

Serena Valand (10)
Longfield Primary School, Harrow

If I Ruled The World...

If I ruled the world,
I would give the poor
A little bit of money,
And maybe some more.

If I ruled the world,
I would stop all the wars,
And help all the injured
And dying off the floors.

If I ruled the world,
I would end all deforestation,
I would give animals a place to live,
With a little more creation.

If only, if only I ruled the world,
I would make the world a better place,
And I would put a smile on everyone's face.

Aaryan Chudasama (9)
Longfield Primary School, Harrow

Sunshine

Sunshine sweeps the clouds away,
Sunshine brightens up the day,
Sunshine chases away the gloom,
From every corner of your room,
Sunshine melts the sadness away,
Sunshine fades away all the grey,
Sitting in the sunshine makes me hum,
Playing in the sunshine makes it fun,
Sunshine gives us light,
It makes the world so bright.
What would I do without sunshine?
What would I do without daytime?

With no sunshine, there is no life!

Saara Ahmed (9)
Longfield Primary School, Harrow

Nature's Truth

Nature's beauty is so fascinating.
It sets you out and makes you free.
As it is to be populating.
Without the cost of even a rupee.

Nature isn't just trees, it's life
It's nothing compared to the wildlife.
Where leaves bloom, so do hopes
It's not so hard to cope.

A massive ray of sunset
Which you won't be able to forget.
A voice roaming about
Being as silent as a mouse.

Nature!

Yug Ruparelia (10)
Longfield Primary School, Harrow

Trees

I don't think I have ever seen
Something as beautiful as a tree

It has shades of green
With leaves swaying in the wind so free

Standing as firm as a queen
Beaming with glee

All the things that I can see
Playful squirrels running free

Providing shelter to not be seen,
For insects, birds and bees.

I don't think I have ever seen
Something as beautiful as a tree.

Zoya Naqshbandi (10)
Longfield Primary School, Harrow

How Beautiful Can Nature Be?

How beautiful can nature be?
All animals are clearly free.
Insects, birds, fish under the sea,
They are all, of course, around me!

Trees here, trees there,
They're all around, and I *do* care.
Our nature is as beautiful as it can be,
Our nature is beautiful, so you see?

We need to take care of it,
As well as we can.
We need to take care of it,
Because it was not made by man.

Roberta Ion (9)
Longfield Primary School, Harrow

The Person Writing My Story

The person writing my story,
Keep her in it,
She's my hero,
You've taken my main
Character away,
But please don't take her.

Without her, I'm nothing,
Without her, I will starve,
Without her, I'm scared in the dark,
Without her, I'm nothing.

The person writing my story,
Keep her in it,
I love her, she is my world.
She is my mother.

Jodele Foster-Wickham (10)
Longfield Primary School, Harrow

Happiness

Happiness can make you smile
At least once in a while
Happiness means a lot to me
Be the best person you can be.

Happiness fills us with hope
Fills us with strength
Fills us with power
Every single hour

Happiness helps us achieve our goal
Helps us fulfil our dream
Helps us get back in control

So, count to three
And decide who you want to be.

Shiven Joshi (10)
Longfield Primary School, Harrow

Stealth Jaguar

A long thick tail that helps to climb trees,
Spots that are there but can never be seen,
It prowls at night with smooth black fur,
Male and female can both roar and purr,
Retractable claws are necessary,
As all of its prey is very furry.
The third largest cat on the Earth.
They will battle intensely to protect their turf.

Night prowler, water dweller, stealth jaguar.

Inayah Khan (10)
Longfield Primary School, Harrow

Ronaldo Is The Best!

Ronaldo
Is my idol
And the
Only GOAT
I know
And
Messi
Send
As
PSG.

Ronaldo is an amazing
Football player, Ronaldo
Won the World Cup
His favourite song's Higher, Higher
Better Together and he is
My favourite football player
Amazing and is my
Significant figure
So, he likes football and I am
Nearly like him.

Shlok Patel (10)
Longfield Primary School, Harrow

My Mind

My mind can travel anywhere
My mind can travel anytime
Like a rocket or a submarine
Into the deep ocean, out of space
My mind filled with hopes and dreams

My wide eyes can see the invisibility
My lonely ears can hear the silence
Sometimes, I think why my mind is like this
My mind is very often in a deep confusion
Wherefore I listen to my heart.

Kairos Sunuwar (9)
Longfield Primary School, Harrow

Why I Like Football

F ootball is my favourite sport,
O h no! The ball was coming towards the goal, thankfully it was caught
O ccasionally, I am on the pitch,
T hank god I didn't step into a ditch.
B ut I am usually goalie,
A fter the match, I eat guacamole.
L ong and friendly is how I like the match,
L ook now, I want a rematch!

Jasmin Sehdev (10)
Longfield Primary School, Harrow

I Don't Bully In School

I don't bully in school
Don't think me a fool

Please don't bully
That will be fool-y

If you cry
We'll make you happy, and we do our best to try

Don't you moan
With the blue zone
'Cause you won't be on your own
I'll get an ice cream with a cone.

Vibha Vikrenth (10)
Longfield Primary School, Harrow

Spring

Spring is here, spring is here,
Goodbye, cold and shiver.
Birds are singing,
Flowers are blooming,
Spring is here, spring is here.
Sun shining bright,
Clear skies and brighter nights,
Spring is here, spring is here.
Red, purple and pink flowers are here,
Spring is here, spring is here.

Hrishi Patel (10)
Longfield Primary School, Harrow

When I Am Queen

When I grow up,
I shall become the queen!
It will take a long path to get there,
With borders in-between.

As quick as lightning,
I will do what I can,
To achieve what I want,
So, now I will start my plan.

Maryam Mafaz (9)
Longfield Primary School, Harrow

The More You Read

The more you read,
The more you know.
The more you know,
The more you can become.
The more you can become,
The more you can succeed.
The more you can succeed,
The more successful you can be.

Selina Parekh (10)
Longfield Primary School, Harrow

The (Other) Nile River

Whoosh, swish, drip, splash
Whoosh, swish, drip, splash
Underground rivers are fast flowing
Underground caves are big.

Slosh, trickle, patter, gush
Slosh, trickle, patter, gush
Fantastic rock formations
Shallow rivers have crawling creatures.

Whoosh, plop, sprinkle, drizzle
Whoosh, plop, sprinkle, drizzle
Black water rafting
Slow-moving currently are flooding floods.

Whoosh, drizzle, splash, plop
Whoosh, drizzle, splash, plop
River system starting source
White cave underground.

Whoosh, plop, sprinkle, drizzle
Whoosh, plop, sprinkle, drizzle
Black water rafting
Slow-moving currents are flooding floods.

Whoosh, drizzle, splash, plop
Whoosh, drizzle, splash, plop
River system starting source
White cave underground.

Merwa Khayyam (8)
St James' CE Primary School, Ashton-Under-Lyne

The Amazon River

Whoosh, swish, drip, splash
Whoosh, swish, drip, splash
Giant river, fast-flowing river
Giant river, bigger than a fast-flowing river.

Trickle, slosh, patter, gush
Trickle, slosh, patter, gush
Bird-eating spiders are more deadly than a poison dart frog
Bird-eating spiders are bigger than a poison dart frog.

Whoosh, swish, drip, splash
Whoosh, swish, drip, splash
Black caimans go faster than fast, big, swimming otters
And black caimans can swim faster than flooding floods.

Trickle, slosh, patter, gush
Trickle, slosh, patter, gush
Amazon region starts a source before the rainforest
The rainforest has flying creatures.

Luca Oncica (8)
St James' CE Primary School, Ashton-Under-Lyne

The New Nile River

Whoosh, swish, drip, splash
Whoosh, swish, drip, splash
Every river starts with a source, then eroding erosion starts
This river has slow-moving currents.

Trickle, slosh, patter, gush
Trickle, slosh, patter, gush
Water rafting, fast-flowing river
Humans gazing at the fascinating rock formations.
Whoosh, swish, drip, splash
Whoosh, swish, drip, splash
People peeking at the dazzling display of glowworms
Floating, fresh water, underground cave beneath you.

Trickle, slosh, patter, gush
Trickle, slosh, patter, gush
Rain can be slightly acidic
Archaeologists have found sacred objects such as creepy creatures.

Rayaan Ashraf (8)
St James' CE Primary School, Ashton-Under-Lyne

The Other Dashing River

Drip, patter, swish, swoosh,
Drip, patter, swish, swoosh,
The rapid river is in New Zealand,
You travel, black water rafting.

Drip, plop, trickle, sprinkle,
Drip, plop, trickle, sprinkle,
There are winding passageways,
The river is an underground river.

Drip, patter, swish, swoosh,
Drip, patter, swish, swoosh,
The river is shallow,
The river has fascinating rock formations.

Drip, trickle, plop, sprinkle,
Drip, trickle, plop, sprinkle,
The river is a subterranean cave with careful currents,
At one point, you are looking at a dazzling display of glow-worms.

Maddison Cook (9)
St James' CE Primary School, Ashton-Under-Lyne

The Nile River

Splash, whoosh, slosh, gurgle
Splash, whoosh, slosh, gurgle
All starts with a source
It naturally forms and gets fast-flowing.

Drip, patter, trickle, plop
Drip, patter, trickle, plop
After all, it meanders, erodes and floods plains
It starts to become a wide river.

Sprinkle, drizzle, drip, gush
Sprinkle, drizzle, drip, gush
Caring communities settle near the river
Very large and a water source.

Splash, whoosh, slosh, gurgle
Splash, whoosh, slosh, gurgle
Goes through eleven African counties with winding winds
World's largest river.

Jayden Verdes (9)
St James' CE Primary School, Ashton-Under-Lyne

The New Nile River

Splash, drip, whoosh, swish
Splash, drip, whoosh, swish
More than twenty underground rivers
Visitors can see the starry sky, countless.

Trickle, sprinkle, gush, drizzle
Trickle, sprinkle, gush, drizzle
Water rafting with creepy creatures
From head bumps to bat droppings.

Plop, whoosh, patter, drip
Plop, whoosh, patter, drip
Earth's longest underground river, fast flowing
Archaeologists have found sacred objects.

Trickle, drizzle, slosh, pop
Trickle, drizzle, slosh, pop
It is New Zealand
Limestone caverns at this river.

Confidence Igwe (9)
St James' CE Primary School, Ashton-Under-Lyne

The Underground River

Swoosh, plop, patter, splash
Swoosh, plop, patter, splash
The glow-worms make a starry-sky entrance
Starts with a source

Whoosh, drop, drizzle, plop
Whoosh, drop, drizzle, plop
From the source to the river.
The meandering river has a dazzling display

Patter, splash, drip, drop
Patter, splash, drip, drop
You'll see fascinating formations of rocks
Caused by wind and water erosion.

Echo, sprinkle, drizzle, plop
Echo, sprinkle, drizzle, plop
Explore the cave in a boat
Twenty more cave systems with crawly creatures.

Abdul Cande (8)
St James' CE Primary School, Ashton-Under-Lyne

The New Nile

Whoosh, trickle, drip, splash
Whoosh, trickle, drip, splash
Slow-flowing currents with a starry sky
In New Zealand

Swish, slosh, patter, gush
Swish, slosh, patter, gush
Rain can slowly be acidic
The river makes underground caves

Plop, sprinkle, drizzle, splash
Plop, sprinkle, drizzle, splash
Some rivers are covered up
Crystal-clear river flows into a subterranean system

Dazzle, sploosh, swoosh, pitter
Dazzle, sploosh, swoosh, pitter
The New Nile has a big display of glowworms
The river is not always clear.

Ume Noreen (9)
St James' CE Primary School, Ashton-Under-Lyne

The Other Nile River

Trickle, splash, patter, gush
Trickle, splash, patter, gush
Starting source, *patter, plop*
Water meandering
Slosh, whoosh, drip, plop

Slosh, whoosh, drip, plop
White water, shallow splash
Slosh, water rafting.
Trickle, splash, patter, gush

Trickle, splash, patter, gush
Rain giving acidic drizzle
Drip from a starry sky.
Slosh, whoosh, drip, plop

Slosh, whoosh, drip, plop
Has slow-moving currents, more than a
Sprinkle, *slosh*, twenty underground, under the city.

Ismail Raza (8)
St James' CE Primary School, Ashton-Under-Lyne

The Amazon River

Splash, swish, drip, trickle
Splash, swish, drip, trickle
Flowing, fresh abundance of water
Travelling from Brazil to Venezuela.

Gush, plop, sprinkle, drip
Gush, plop, sprinkle, drip
Warm area with creepy creatures
Amazonian people live near the river.

Splash, swish, drip, trickle
Splash, swish, drip, trickle
Lonely, long, fresh river
Carrying water to the Atlantic.

Gush, plop, sprinkle, drip
Gush, plop, sprinkle, drip
There are amazing, warm waves
The cute, giant river otters.

Hannah Moyhuddin (9)
St James' CE Primary School, Ashton-Under-Lyne

The (Other) Nile River

Whoosh, swish, drip, splash
Whoosh, swish, drip, splash
Underground rivers are fast flowing
Underground caves are big

Slosh, trickle, patter, gush
Slosh, trickle, patter, gush
Fantastic rock formations
Shallow rivers have crawling creatures.

Whoosh, plop, sprinkle, drizzle
Whoosh, plop, sprinkle, drizzle
Black water rafting
Slow-moving currents are flooding floods.

Whoosh, drizzle, splash, plop
Whoosh, drizzle, splash, plop
River system starting source
White cave underground.

Zainab Ehsan (9)
St James' CE Primary School, Ashton-Under-Lyne

The Nile

Splish, gush, patter, drizzle
Splish, gush, patter, drizzle
Starts with a source
The Nile and Amazon are rival running rivers.

Slosh, plop, patter, splash
Slosh, plop, patter, splash
Flowing flood plains
Terrifying, twisting, shifting river.

Plop, splish, sprinkle, splash
Plop, splish, sprinkle, splash
Flowing fast, meandering
Several rivers could challenge.

Splash, gush, drizzle, slosh
Splash, gush, drizzle, slosh
The Nile was an important route
For exciting Egyptians.

Olivia Kenyon (9)
St James' CE Primary School, Ashton-Under-Lyne

The Second Nile River

Whoosh, swish, drip, swoosh
Whoosh, swish, drip, swoosh
Dripping and flowing
Underground caves.

Gush, drizzle, plop, drip
Gush, drizzle, plop, drip
Crystals all around and light
Crystal-clear and lightning shining.

Splash, drizzle, pop, gush
Splash, drizzle, pop, gush
Rainwater sleeps in soil
Rain can be slightly acidic

Splash, plop, gush, pop
Splash, plop, gush, pop
Unaware fact of twenty
Rivers can be meandering.

Ziad Bowden (9)
St James' CE Primary School, Ashton-Under-Lyne

The Amazing Nile

Patter, trickle, gush, slosh
Patter, trickle, gush, slosh
Starting at a source
I get faster and faster.

Drop, sprinkle, drip, patter
Drop, sprinkle, drip, patter
Meanders and meanders
Eroding the land.

Gush, slosh, trickle, patter
Gush, slosh, trickle, patter
Humans settle near me
I get very wide.

Splash, whoosh, slosh, gush
Splash, whoosh, slosh, gush
Go through many countries
The longest river in the world.

Oscar Carr (9)
St James' CE Primary School, Ashton-Under-Lyne

Nile In New Zealand

Patter, sprinkle, splash, tinkle,
The New Nile river is in New Zealand,
It starts with a source,
With crawling creatures.

Gush, drip, clop, plop,
Slow-moving currents,
There's black and white water,
You can always see glowworms on the fantastic formations.

Trickle, swish, patter, pop,
A cave system that is large,
Winding rivers always meander,
The rocks shine like a dazzling display.

Splash, whoosh, tinkle, gush,
Constant dripping causes frustration,
The shallow river is crystal clear,
Fascinating formations will surely stop you in your tracks!

Ubaid Mirza (9)
St James' CE Primary School, Ashton-Under-Lyne

River Lifestyle

Slosh, whoosh, swish, drip
Slosh, whoosh, swish, drip
Nile and Amazon are
Rival running rivers.

Trickle, slosh, patter, gush
Trickle, slosh, patter, gush
Start source, flood, flowing
Several rivers could challenge
The record.

Plop, sprinkle, drizzle, gush
Plop, sprinkle, drizzle, gush
Every year, the river floods
Flood plain.

Splash, patter, gush, drip
Splash, patter, gush, drip
Egypt still lives near the
Nile.

Imaan Shahzad (9)
St James' CE Primary School, Ashton-Under-Lyne

New Zealand

Drip, drip, drip, drip
Drip, drip, drip, drip
The souse of the river
Fast falling down

Swish, drip, bang, bang
Swish, drip, bang, bang
Crystals all around and light
Crystal clear and lightning shining

Clank, clank, clank, clank
Clank, clank, clank, clank
Sacrifices happening everywhere
Underground creatures come

Drip, drip, drip, drip
Drip, drip, drip, drip
Chambers everywhere
Same with limestone.

Awaais Rashid (8)
St James' CE Primary School, Ashton-Under-Lyne

The (Other) Nile River

Whoosh, drip, swish, splash
Whoosh, drip, swish, splash
Looking up at a dazzling display
Unlike white water, fast flowing.

Slosh, trickle, patter, gush
Slosh, trickle, patter, gush
Water creates underground caves
Diver finds it crystal clear down in fresh water.

Whoosh, plop, sprinkle, drizzle
Whoosh, plop, sprinkle, drizzle
Animals and human bones
Fast-flowing, winding passageway.

Haleema Mahmood (9)
St James' CE Primary School, Ashton-Under-Lyne

The New Nile

Drip, drip, swoosh, plop
Black water rafting is a fun way to explore
Drip, drip, swoosh, plop
The New Nile is in New Zealand

Drip, drip, swoosh, plop
A dazzling display of glow-worms
Drip, drip, swoosh, plop
The water is very shallow

Drip, drip, swoosh, plop
Helmets keep you safe for head bumps and bat poo
Drip, drip, swoosh, plop
It's a shiny sea full of jellyfish.

Lana Jamal (9)
St James' CE Primary School, Ashton-Under-Lyne

The Amazon River

Whoosh, wash, drip, splash,
Whoosh, wash, drip, splash,
The river is fast-flowing
Plants are getting water

Gush, patter, drizzle, plop,
Gush, patter, drizzle, plop,
Animals are eating
Animals are hunting

Trickle, sprinkle, splosh, slush
Trickle, sprinkle, splosh, slush
Creepy creatures
Many animals like a gold lion.

Ismail Mohammed (9)
St James' CE Primary School, Ashton-Under-Lyne

The (Other) Nile River

Swish, plop, drip, gush
Swish, plop, drip, gush
Every river starts with a source
Dazzling display of ancient bones.

Swish, plop, drip, gush
Swish, plop, drip, gush
Slow-moving currents
Fast-forming erosion happens

Swish, plop, drip, gush
Swish, plop, drip, gush.

Zara Vaughan (8)
St James' CE Primary School, Ashton-Under-Lyne

The Nile River

Drip, drip, drip, drip
Drip, drip, drip, drip
Fast-flowing river systems
Covered and built over.

Drip, drip, drip, drip
Drip, drip, drip, drip
White-water London.

Drip, drip, drip, drip
Drip, drip, drip, drip
Terrific transportation begins from white water.

Roman Ramezan (9)
St James' CE Primary School, Ashton-Under-Lyne

Amazing Forest River

Amazing forest river
Drip, drip, drip, drip,
6,400, 5.5 million square kilometres.
Chaotic currents.

Drip, drip, drip, drip,
Drip, drip, drip, drip,
A rare chance of an endless wave
Mammals.

Freddie Peaterson (9)
St James' CE Primary School, Ashton-Under-Lyne

The Dragon's History

Dragons are normally *dangerous* mythical creatures,
But this one has very different features.
After her family has been taken from the Englishmen,
She lies inside her family's den.
While she's lying down, thinking about her and her friends.
Could this be the very end?
Sitting there, can't stop crying,
When she looks out, she sees other dragons flying.
She decides to join the pack,
And maybe get her family back?
She decided to go with them, with a smile on her face,
And then they were gone, *poof*, without a trace
And that's the end, the dragon's history
But who knows? It might be a mystery.

Myra Lepcha Shaw (9)
St Mary Redcliffe CE Primary School, Windmill Hill

The Fox In The Forest

Dark orange body and browny-white tail,
Flame-red eyes, but whose is this trail?
Sticking-up ears and snowy-blank paws,
The urge to explore and hunt with those jaws.
Trapped in a cave, not allowed to go out,
Because his grandparents were lost, with a very big doubt...
Stuck in this cave, day after day,
Sat by the fire as he's told to obey.
But one winter's night, our small little fox,
Snuck out of that cage, under a box.
He snuck through the forest and discovered another cave,
Crept right in, saw his grandparents, while trying to be brave!
Then he said, "*I thought you were dead!*"
They walked towards him and replied,
"No, we're not, did you try to hide?"
He started to cry, then started to stutter,
"It's my parents!" he wailed and began to mutter.

He ran out the cave to see his mum and dad,
When he explained, they were ever so glad.
They rushed to him, smiled and played hide-and-seek,
With a big, furry bear, for what felt like a week!
And that, my friend, is the end of our story,
Of a curious fox and all of his glory!

Isobel Brown (9)
St Mary Redcliffe CE Primary School, Windmill Hill

Africa Song

Down in Africa, where the rains never fall,
From the pounding of lions hunting down deer,
To the yelling yells of hyenas, and
Deep in the heart of Africa
You can hear the deafening trumpeting herds of elephants.

When you wake up,
You can hear the hawking, squawking of the African grey parrots
And then down, up and late,
You can hear the munching of beautiful giraffes.
When you go down to the bay,
You can see the splashing of African penguins.

When you get up close,
You can hear the sweet purr of cheetahs,
You can see the stumbling rhinos charging behind the setting golden sun
And down by the watering hole, you see the hippos lying by the bank.

Now it's late in the boiling sun, you see the magical serval leaping right in front of you
And then, when you go deep into the forest,
You see leopards creeping up on warthogs
And the beautiful white and black stripes of zebra herds.

Jonah Smith (8) & Juliet Croft (8)
St Mary Redcliffe CE Primary School, Windmill Hill

My Book Of Life

From the moment I first opened my eyes,
And my eyelids started to blink,
I made memories,
Had dreams and...
Smiled
This was love...
I think

Lying in my cot at night,
Being scared of old Saint Nick
Screaming,
Crying,
Laughing,
Singing,
Until a page of my book went
Flick

When my whole world split in two,
And my parents lost their 'woohoo'
There was screaming over the
Telephone,

That's when I started to feel...
Alone

As I grew older and began to
S p r e a d
My wings,
I found a love for sewing.
Then things started to reach
Uphill.
The bad times were going.

Now, as my life enters a new chapter,
And I know I have loved ones around me,
When I start to swim in a larger lake,
They'll always be there for tea.

Evie Rose Henry (11)
St Mary Redcliffe CE Primary School, Windmill Hill

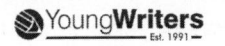

A Mother's Love

Dedicated to my mum

Will you be better in six months?
I ask Mum when she starts chemo,
"Soon," she says

Will you be better in five months?
I ask Mum as her beautiful
Locks fall out.
"Soon," she says

Will you be better in four months?
I ask Mum as she starts radiotherapy,
"Soon," she says.

Will you be better in three months?
I ask as she vomits into a bowl.
But this time, she doesn't reply
Will you be better someday?
I cry.
"Yes, yes," she says as small
Baby hairs start
Growing.

Sasha Penman (11)
St Mary Redcliffe CE Primary School, Windmill Hill

Two Souls As One

Once together, now apart,
Two souls separated by a dart.
This place isn't my home and it never will be,
Not without that one person who makes me, me.

Same mother, same father, two brothers as one,
But now when I look over my shoulder,
I see none.
The safety I have I can't take for granted,
For I know people like you aren't so enchanted.

People are building a life just for me,
But I can't settle in whilst you're over sea.
I hope I see you again some day,
Any price I'm willing to pay.

Scarlet Porter (11), Megan Harvey (11) & Megan Anthony (11)
St Mary Redcliffe CE Primary School, Windmill Hill

Nothing But War

Bombs dropping night and day,
My village a terrifying display,

Nothing can stop what has begun,
Just sadness now, no more fun,

Half the village, they have fled,
The others, who knows, alive or dead?

Under cover I have to lie,
As the planes fill the sky,

My heart is full of despair and grief,
My home, my life, is empty of belief,

I stood at the peer, waving goodbye,
My friends, my family, would they die?

No hope, no home, no friends,
Has my life begun to end?

Amelie Williams (11) & Audrey Gibbard (11)
St Mary Redcliffe CE Primary School, Windmill Hill

Nature

The wild is wonderful, even the trees.
You respect the animals, even the bees.
Nature is great, nature is wild.
My advice to you is stay as a child.
But scientists still haven't
Seen all the creatures.
Or much, yes, not
Much or all of their features.
Now I have finished my
Wonderful speech.
And I
Hope it was enough to teach
You all about nature, through
And through.
If you need more
Information, go to the zoo!

Emilia Turner (9) & Shameika Sappleton (9)
St Mary Redcliffe CE Primary School, Windmill Hill

When You Left

When you left, my whole life changed,
Just one bullet sent you away.
There's a place in my heart where you used to stand
But now, when I look, you're nowhere to be found.
My love for you will stay forever,
Forgetting you I will never.
The one in front of the gun lives forever, they say
But, to me, it doesn't seem that way.
I will never forgive the person who took you away
'Cause my only wish is that you would stay.

Salwa Caraye (10), Hamda & Scarlet Porter (11)
St Mary Redcliffe CE Primary School, Windmill Hill

Wonderful Weather

Whether the weather is rainy or sunny
The weather can sometimes be a bit funny
The weather can sometimes do two things at once
I like when it's raining and bright
It makes a rainbow full of light
When it's cold and snowing
And everything's glowing
The snowflakes fall down from the sky
We throw snowballs up so high
Whether the weather is hot or cold
It's always a sight to behold.

Clio Mongon (9)
St Mary Redcliffe CE Primary School, Windmill Hill

Winter Weekends

Winter weekends
Are a time to
Rest,
To cosy up
With a book and
Be our best,
With blankets and
Pillows, we'll be
Blessed,
And let
The world outside
Take a rest.

You can hear the creak, squeak,
You open your mouth to fill up with warmth,
Hot cocoa is chocolatey and
Creamy, all the marshmallows
Float in the hot cocoa
Like a pond. *Yum!*

Maisey-Jade Arthur Brooks (11)
St Mary Redcliffe CE Primary School, Windmill Hill

Road's End

Subtle, strange, not really real,

I don't know what to ask, I don't know what
To feel,

I could take him to the station, it's not that
Far,

I could take him there, in my brand-new
Car,

The man's face is covered, his eyes unseen,
Then his head starts to lean,

I look into his goggles and see my fate,
Then I realise it's too late!

Amelie Williams (11)
St Mary Redcliffe CE Primary School, Windmill Hill

Ponies And Horses

Something pulls me close to you,
My life has to be about you,
How could I ever be without you?
All my years I've saved up for you,
I would give my life up for you,
All my years I'll spend with you,
Will bring me even closer to you,
There's only one thing I'll ever call this,
'Cause you'll always be my baby horses,
Now that's my special message for you.

Minna Kauntze (9)
St Mary Redcliffe CE Primary School, Windmill Hill

Rulers Of The Sky!

They come in all shapes and sizes, but are always the same.
Our world would *never* be one if they had never come.
They've always been here and they'll always be with us.
The feathers which cover their wings are truly mysterious.
They can fly through the air or stride with pride.
They have feathers and beaks, but are certainly not mammals.

What are they?
Why, they're birds!

Evan Cormack (9)
St Mary Redcliffe CE Primary School, Windmill Hill

Save The Earth

Let's save the Earth, our planet so dear,
For the animals and plants, and people living here.
We can turn off all the lights, when we're not in the room,
And walk and ride our bikes to reduce all the fumes.
We can recycle and reuse to cut down on our waste!
Let's be kind to the Earth every single day,
And remember that it's worthy in every single way!

Ta'Shiyah Douglas (9)
St Mary Redcliffe CE Primary School, Windmill Hill

Poppies

I opened my eyes and death is unleashed all around me.
Hope faded into nothingness, what I thought was real seemed to be an illusion.
Huge metal monsters were taking everything with them
Leaving their victims behind them.
Souls seemed as if they were freed from the wretched imprisonment of life.
But one thing reassured me, the sea of poppies around me.

Maggie Wilshire & Iona Miller (11)
St Mary Redcliffe CE Primary School, Windmill Hill

Death

Death, it's like a snake, once on the victim, twice
On the poison.
Like grief, once extreme, second a slow, powerful
Killer blow.
Death some do
Death some stop
Some people handle it
Some don't let go
But those with grief must be cared
For so
Those could do with support, ya know.

Caolan (10)
St Mary Redcliffe CE Primary School, Windmill Hill

The Tragedy Of War

T he tragedy of war turns the world inside out,
R efugees run from the dropping bombs and bullets,
O ff the land that they loved,
O ff without their family or friends,
P lease stop before the world turns from calm to panic,
S top before everything... is gone.

Barnaby Watson (8)
St Mary Redcliffe CE Primary School, Windmill Hill

Oceans

Oceans shimmer and shine.
They go far out you can't see
Some magic parts.
The sea is magic because it
Remembers everything.
There are creatures you don't
Know about yet.
They might be big and tough
Or small and weak.
But only
The sea
Knows.

Stella Simson (8)
St Mary Redcliffe CE Primary School, Windmill Hill

Snoring Brothers

I woke in the morning
In my awning
To the sound of my brother snoring
It was a hot, sunny day
And it was time to play
But all I could hear was him yawning
I boiled an egg
I chopped a leg
But still, he was snoring
And yawning!

Juliet Croft (8)
St Mary Redcliffe CE Primary School, Windmill Hill

Words Can Hurt Too!

Words have meanings, they can
Hurt too.
They can't punch and kick, but they can burn
You.
They leave holes in your heart that can never
Be filled
It's like being stabbed in the chest
Before you've been killed.

Megan Anthony (11)
St Mary Redcliffe CE Primary School, Windmill Hill

I Want To Go To The Seaside

I love the seaside
The waves are big
They splash and they crash

I love the seaside
It is calm, it is fun
Ice cream like from a dream

I love the seaside
The blue sky
The salty sea and me.

Anya Clements (7)
St Mary Redcliffe CE Primary School, Windmill Hill

Skyward-Bound Dragon

I fly up high in the sky,
It is in my nature to never lie.

As I fly, I soar and roar,
I am more than just an old lore.

People think I collect numerous things,
But all I need are my two wings.

Ophelia Bell (11)
St Mary Redcliffe CE Primary School, Windmill Hill

The Wonderful Wild

The wonderful wild has tall, long trees
The wonderful wild is just for me
I dream of the air so crisp and clean
It's filled with animals that have not been seen
My wonderful world is so amazing.

Stevie Rogers (8)
St Mary Redcliffe CE Primary School, Windmill Hill

Cookies!

Full of chocolate chips
Made with love and care
These yummy things,
Could melt in your mouth,
Or crumble as you eat it
These delicious entities
Are the final piece in life.

Isaac Couzens (10)
St Mary Redcliffe CE Primary School, Windmill Hill

Fire

Roaring, blasting,
Spreading like a virus,
As a demon kills,
You must pay the bills,
Fire is finishing.

Sebastian Flower (11)
St Mary Redcliffe CE Primary School, Windmill Hill

The Light Is Bright

The light is bright
Just like my night
And I will always fight for right.
East or west
You are best.

Veda (9)
St Mary Redcliffe CE Primary School, Windmill Hill

Seasons

Springtime
Flowers blooming
Plants and seeds are forming
Trees are tall and fruits are growing
Sunrise
Sun is shining
It's a hot paradise
The sun is high in the blue sky
Sunshine
Autumn
Autumn is here
Leaves are changing colours
Leaves turn crispy brown, then they fall
Christmas
Snow is falling
The cold season is here
Days are getting shorter, shorter
Freezing.

Sarah Pegg (10)
Stalham Academy, Stalham

My Favourite Animal ~ Could You Guess?

I am scaly and long,
Feisty and strong
I stay at lakes in South America.
I like meat, it's such an amazing treat
There are many nearby.
My eyes glow, letting people know I'm nearby,
When I'm near, people are in fear
And they...
Run, run, run, run, run, run away,
Whilst I stay.

Can you guess my animal?

Answer: An alligator.

Tommy Austrin (9)
Stalham Academy, Stalham

Manchester United

Manchester United
Good club
Destroying every club
FA Cup winners
Europa Cup winners

Some of the best players in the team are -
Casemiro, De Gea, Rashford,
Antony, Varane,
Luke Shaw, and Bruno Fernandes.

Legends of the club include -
David Beckham, Bryan Robson, Paul Scholes,
Wayne Rooney, Roy Keane,
George Best and Edwin van der Sar.

Max Tansley (9)
Stalham Academy, Stalham

The Book Of Your Dreams

Have you ever wondered
If there's a perfect book?
Well, it's not like you can just look,
You might think there's no such thing
Well, that is my dream, to create a dream book so...
Bing!
You would not believe that someone has thought about your dream
So, my goal is for the dreams that are a seam
To be - broken!

Lily Terrington (10)
Stalham Academy, Stalham

My Magical Forest

Through the fence, there is a magical forest.
Branches everywhere, leaves on the floor
And moss on the logs.
All I can hear are birds tweeting and the crunch of
the branches on the floor
And all we have to do is open that wooden door
We need to get through the branches and things if
we want to see more
Of the magic, get to the forest core.

Ally Mcclenaghan (9)
Stalham Academy, Stalham

Nature Queen

Mother Nature is calm,
Mother Nature does bless,
But Mother Nature doesn't have time to rest,

Mother Nature is harsh,
Mother Nature is cruel,
But Mother Nature shall forever and always rule,

Mother Nature is happy,
Mother Nature is jolly,
But Mother Nature can sometimes be a wally!

Maddie Fisher (10)
Stalham Academy, Stalham

Life

When I grow up, I want to be a vet
Even though that job is quite hard to get,
I love to ride my horse, Sparrow, in the summer
Because that is so much funner.
I also am a gymnast, I have been doing hobbies since four,
I can do a backflip right across the floor
And jump over jumps with my horse.

Florence Perrins (9)
Stalham Academy, Stalham

Liverpool

Down the wing
Salah
Goalkeeper and diving
Alisson
Excellent defender
Van Dijk
Great captain
Henderson
The winning manager
Klopp
You'll never walk alone

Trophies
Champions League
Premier League
FA Cup
Europa Cup.

Kaiden Chippindale (9)
Stalham Academy, Stalham

What Am I?

I give you lots of mess to clean,
I will jump and knock you down,
I will watch you for hours,
I can wear you out,
I will make you laugh,
I will make you cry,
I have sharp teeth,
But I will not bite.
What am I?

Answer: A dog.

Matilda Addy (10)
Stalham Academy, Stalham

The Fabulous Waxham Sands!

You can relax on the sand
On a hot summer's day.
You can play and swim
In the water and have
Lots of fun.
You can play with your
Dog.
You can eat ice cream
You can play on the equipment
You can go to the shop.

Ruby Hughes (10)
Stalham Academy, Stalham

Manchester City/Sport

Manchester City
Premier League champs
Manager Pep Guardiola
One of the best
Destroying other teams
FA Cup winners
Back in the days
Erling Haaland
Fifty-two goals in 2023
Which is insane
They are
Insane.

Harvey Mackin (9)
Stalham Academy, Stalham

Scooter

S uperman, whip, name a trick,
C ore is best, get a deck.
O utstanding tricks
O r core deck and bars make you fly,
T ry land a trick,
E xcellent nothing front.
R ide to get good.

Finlay Whittaker-Benson (10)
Stalham Academy, Stalham

Willow

A cute, small, grey cat
Prancing and hunting
Catching loads of mice
Cuddling me all night
She lies on my pillow
Plays with me outside
I love her lots
She is my flower
So fluffy and cute
Playing with you.

Erin Woolston (10)
Stalham Academy, Stalham

Time And Relative Dimension In Space

T ime is a very important thing.
A nd it must be spent well.
R elative means connected and compared to something.
D imensions are out of this world.
I n space.
S o, this is the end.

Jimmy Thrower (9)
Stalham Academy, Stalham

Bars

B est tricks, name your best
A mazing scooter designs, core deck, envy discs, van grips
R iding, make sure to angle your feet at a 90-degree angle
S cooting is so fun and please wear protection.

Archie Coman (9)
Stalham Academy, Stalham

Garden Games

My dogs
Clever, crazy
Running, panting, loving.
We always play ball together
Go fetch!

Outside
Cool, warm, breezy
Chilly, sunny
I go outside when it's sunny
So fun!

Amelia Hudson (10)
Stalham Academy, Stalham

Nature

Sunsets
Pretty, lovely
Glimmering, sparkling
I love seeing great sunsets
Nice view

Flowers,
Beautiful and blue
All here for you!
Leaves, smooth and green
So perfectly clean!

Isabella Fox (9)
Stalham Academy, Stalham

My Odd Thoughts

Sometimes I feel like I need to be a tree,
If I ruled the world, I'd do it with glee,
In the future, I'd like to see me sailing by the sea,
And now I'm hungry for just one pea.

Thomas Jackson (10)
Stalham Academy, Stalham

Pollution's Place

P rotect the fish, the
O ceans too
L et them
L ive
U ntil
T he world
I s healed
O ceans and land
N eed help.

Corey Taylor (10)
Stalham Academy, Stalham

Me And My Friends

Me and my friends
All together
Friends, friends forever.
We share and care
And love each other
We really do care for
One another.

Friends until
The end.

Freya Cooper (9)
Stalham Academy, Stalham

Candles

Candles
Burning, melting, shrinking.
If I were a candle, I would light up the room.
If I were a candle, I would guide you.
Burning, melting, shrinking.
Candles!

Shayla Jarmey (9)
Stalham Academy, Stalham

Fabulous Animals

Cat, cute
Fluffy, playing
I like playing with fluffy cats.
Love cats

Cheetah
Running, eating
I like watching big cats playing
Hunting.

George Grady (10)
Stalham Academy, Stalham

My Love

R uby's eyes are so beautiful,
U nderstanding Ruby is so pretty,
B eautiful Ruby has a cool personality,
Y ou are my world.

Harry Hyde (10)
Stalham Academy, Stalham

Hello Kitty

There was a little kitty
That was a little silly.
But said hello and was named Hello Kitty
She has a friend called Cinnamoroll, it's a bunny.

Emmerson Frost (10)
Stalham Academy, Stalham

When I Grow Up

When I grow up, I would be you
Even if I'm short or tall
Even if I'm not that smart
When I grow up, I would be just like you.

Isabella Cossey (10)
Stalham Academy, Stalham

Animals

Animals
Cake, fun
Chickens, parrots
Amazing, cute, remarkable
Birds, guinea pigs, dogs, cats, snakes, mice
Enjoyment.

Wilbur Dodd (9)
Stalham Academy, Stalham

Demons

D emons
E vil
M alicious
O pposite of good
N ever go near one
S tay away.

Amy Fearn (10)
Stalham Academy, Stalham

The Best Game

Football,
Is the best game,
The best sport in the world,
And I will cheer the boys in blue,
Tractors.

Megan Mace (10)
Stalham Academy, Stalham

Top Corner

Football
Football is good
Football is the best sport
Football is the best sport to me
Top corner.

Logan Wood (10)
Stalham Academy, Stalham

Racing

Racing
Fastest, speeding
Pitting, speaking, winning
Lots of loops around a race track
Winners.

Tyler Clarke (10)
Stalham Academy, Stalham

Friendship

Friendship
Amazing times
Never-forgotten times
Fun, love, jokes, support, memories
Friendship.

Brooke Beales (9)
Stalham Academy, Stalham

Rummage

Amazing
I love him so much
He is my doggy best friend
My adorable companion
Love you!

Olive Nichols (10)
Stalham Academy, Stalham

Sandstorm

Sandstorm
Brave, kind, happy
Daring, helping, staying
She is always prepared
Amazing.

Sophia Bell (9)
Stalham Academy, Stalham

My Dog, Charlie

Charlie
He is so old
I love him all the time
He is so calm around people
Playful.

Mia Eglington (10)
Stalham Academy, Stalham

Norwich

Norwich
Winning, losing
The yellow and green team
The unbeatable Canaries
City!

Archie Harvey (10)
Stalham Academy, Stalham

Oreo, My Guinea Pig

Oreo
Nippy, gorgeous
Fantastic, cute, funny
Outstanding, amazing, sweet
Fun!

Hazel Smith (9)
Stalham Academy, Stalham

Beautiful Bunnies

Bunnies
Soft and fluffy
Extremely cuddly
They are so adorably cute
Rabbits.

Jessica Sharp (10)
Stalham Academy, Stalham

Fortnite

Fortnite
Fast, furious
Brilliant, exciting
I feel happy and excited
Gamer.

Charlie-Jordan Beales (10)
Stalham Academy, Stalham

Historical Raiders

Vikings
Historical
Fearsome barbarians
Danish, fearsome attackers
Raiders.

Benjamin Hobbs (9)
Stalham Academy, Stalham

Cats!

Cats
Adorable
Playful and supportive
Fierce, fast, mouse-catching
Kitty.

Jessie Vaughan (10)
Stalham Academy, Stalham

The Way Of The Tiger

Through the depths of the night lurks
The great beast itself, pure pearl-white fur
And midnight-black stripes that strike fear
In your heart.

Its eyes are sapphire-blue like the reflection
Of a million diamonds in the moonlight
Shimmering on a graceful lake.
The tiger's teeth are as sharp as a shark's and can
Bite through almost anything it wants.

Its claws are as sharp as daggers and
Can slice a rock in half.

And that's the
Way of the
Tiger...

Lyndsey Bourne (10)
Tregadillett Primary School, Tregadillett

Demonic Rabbits

My love of rabbits is very strong
I've had one myself for very long
But, as I grew up, I found out their secrets
At night, they turn into demonic creatures
Even though I know this, I still don't fear
But always, at night, banging I hear

Into the forest they run
And soon, they transform
Into the demonic creatures they are
Their eyes are red
And their fur is black
Soon, they will come to capture you.

Julia Kaletha (9)
Tregadillett Primary School, Tregadillett

Saving Our Planet

E veryone should care,
N o one should be ruining it, it's not fair.
V ital and green
I mportant as anything could be!
R ecycle and reuse as much as you can.
O nly we can make a plan.
N ow it's the time.
M aking up your mind.
E veryone can help.
N ever exclude yourself
T o save our environment!

Lena Pidgeon (9)
Tregadillett Primary School, Tregadillett

What Is Family?

F amily: when you think about family, what do you see?
A dventurous family perhaps?
M aybe you love family time?
I 'm an only child, but you might have brothers or sisters?
L oving family, with pets maybe?
Y ou have a perfect family, whoever you are. Such as two mums or two dads, but what matters is they love you.

Evie Massey (10)
Tregadillett Primary School, Tregadillett

Ghost World

Once a world full of light,
Now a deep and eerie fright.
Terrifying ghosts and entities roam,
No more tranquillity or home.
Dreadful shadows lurking in the dark,
A world with no spark.
Hope seems lost in this haunting place,
Fear and gloom forever in its embrace.
May some daylight return,
And this world no more to burn.

Jason Langdale (9)
Tregadillett Primary School, Tregadillett

The Isle Of Man!

I sland: the Isle of Man is a small island and it will always be home.

S easide: since it is an island, there are beaches everywhere and that can only mean one thing, ice cream! But be careful around the seagulls, they can be feisty.

L axey: pass the famous Laxey Wheel which is the largest working water wheel in the world.

E llan Vannin: this means Isle of Man in Manx/Gaelic. The Isle of Man has its own language, but English people discovered it and the Manx language wasn't used.

O cean: as you know, the sea was everywhere. But the creatures that were in it were interesting. These were animals like jellyfish, seals, dolphins and even basking sharks, which are the second-largest fish growing as long as forty feet and weighing over five tons.

F enella Beach: this is a small beach surrounding the one and only Peel Castle. Back when the Celts were around, they built Peel Castle and used it to protect them. It is still standing to this day.

M oddey Dhoo: this black dog was a mythical horror and scary to everyone. As you walk into Peel Castle, you see a sculpture of him. In the story, people say that the Moddey Dhoo killed a drunk man and was never seen again.

A nimals: many animals are on the Isle of Man. The common seagull is the most annoying, the rarest is the Manx cat with no tail. This is just the result of how the DNA is. Not all cats on the Isle of Man have no tail.

N ursery: Busy Bears and Playgroup are the two nurseries that were in Peel. I went to both. My auntie works at Playgroup and it is the same building as the church.

Elodie Harding (10)
Walmley Junior School, Sutton Coldfield

The Present

Hello, my name is Lexi.
Just to say, I do really like Pepsi!
Keep it away from me, please!
One day, if I have too much, I'll probably get a disease.
Now, this is about the present I got.
You're lucky my mum reminded me or else I would have forgot!
So, it was the 5th of June,
The day before my birthday, it's really true!
I was just texting my friends, but I heard a noise and then, you wouldn't believe it,
It was my mum whispering, "Leave it!"
Who was she talking to? A cat? A man?
Maybe one of her fans?
There was also rustling and ruffling!
Scratches and scrapes!
My mum loudly whispered, "Stop it, grape!"
Grape? I needed to investigate!

I said to myself, "I'm going to find out what this
grape is! Right now, right here!"
But my dad shouted, "Let's grab some beer!"
My mum agreed and locked the door.
I felt like I was going to roar!
Soon, I had to go to bed,
I probably would forget
About the weird, unusual present.
It was suddenly very early,
I felt something very slobby, like wet coffee.
It was a cute brown puppy!
I was very lucky,
That was the present I had,
I am really, really glad!

Isabella Jagroo (9)
Walmley Junior School, Sutton Coldfield

Loving Family

In a cosy little house,
Lived a loving family of five,
With parents and siblings,
They made each day come alive.

Together, they laughed and played,
Sharing memories sweet and true,
They hold hands and hug tight,
In everything they do.

The mom cooked up tasty meals,
The dad read stories out loud,
The kids played with toys and games,
And danced to music extremely loud.

They went on picnics and hikes,
And watched the stars at night,
They supported each other's dreams,
And made everything feel just right.

In this family full of love,
No one ever felt alone,
They had each other's dreams,
And a place they called their own.

And so, this poem is written,
To all the families near and far,
May your love for each other,
Shine brighter than all the stars.

Cindy Ding (9)
Walmley Junior School, Sutton Coldfield

Our Farm

We have a pig that likes to dig.
We also have an owl that likes to growl.
We have a few cats that hunt down the rats.
We have a goat with a lovely white coat.
All these animals are so much fun, grazing in the meadows until the day is done.
Back to the barns they gently lie in, the soft golden hay to sleep back in.
Now, off they go up and away, back to the meadows where they like to play.
In the meadows full of flowers, there are many trees as high as towers.
There is also a little cow, so you better make him listen now.
In the night sky, there are rocket ships that go very high.
The animals like to jump in puddles whilst being in massive huddles.
Now it is the end of the day, we've said all the things we were meant to say.
Thank you for listening to all we've said, now we must go to bed.

Elora Sallis (8) & Tilly Soesan (9)
Walmley Junior School, Sutton Coldfield

My Dream Mansion

D ream houses are cool and they're the best!
R isky waterslides and pony rides, I never rest!
E aster time in my house, I love it!
A nd I don't sit down, it's legit!
M agical and merry, I don't need money! A miraculous beehive, the bees give me honey

M ansions are major and majestic!
A nd I'm always so energetic
N uggets and nachos I always eat!
S tuff I always use, it's never obsolete!
I 'm really gregarious
O h, this mansion has various
N ature all around here, I'm prominent and able to drive, that really wasn't clear.

Pihu Bhalla (7)
Walmley Junior School, Sutton Coldfield

Nature

N ature is a magnificent part of life.
A nimals are a big part of nature as well. Without animals, nature might not exist.
T he reason why we need nature is because without it our world wouldn't be beautiful and filled with wildlife.
U niverse is filled with nature. Did you know that trees, plants, animals and humans are a massive part of nature too?
R esponsible people will take care of nature and you should too!
E very single animal in the universe is very important to nature, if we kill animals, we kill wildlife.

Nature, nature is a beautiful thing,
Sometimes it is so nice, it makes you want to sing!

Eloise George (9) & Talia Matar (9)
Walmley Junior School, Sutton Coldfield

I Love Nature

Bluebells are blue, blueberries I like to chew.
I love nature, I hope you do too.
I love the way the tall brown trees sway in the breeze.
I love the way the stripy buzzy bees buzz in the breeze.
I love the small, quiet, colourful butterflies fluttering above my head, as I lie on nature as a bed.
I love the way the fluffy bunnies hop in the long green grass, as squirrels run so fast.
The ocean is silky blue, I love the ocean, how about you?
I love the way the shiny grey dolphins jump and play in the deep blue sea,
I love the way the deep green turtles swim about at the bottom of the sea.
Nature is beautiful, hope you think so too!

Poppy Bowen (7)
Walmley Junior School, Sutton Coldfield

Lots Of Different Animals

Animals to you look very, very sweet,
but sometimes they are things that we actually eat.

Some animals we own, like a dog or a cat,
but they can actually make a very dirty mat.

Animals live in lots of different places, some of them are warm, some of them are nice,
but even I know animals that live by the cold ice.

Animals have different colours like yellow, black or brown,
but some of them might be the kings and really wear a crown.

Elephants live in deserts where it's hot and nice and sunny,
but I hope you do not kill them for a little bit of money.

Eva Beauchamp (9)
Walmley Junior School, Sutton Coldfield

Edith's Marvellous Medicine

Just gulp it down and have no fear.
"How do you like it, Granny dear?"
Will she go *pop* like a jack-in-the-box?
Start growling like an angry fox?
Will she start smelling like a mouldy sock?
Start ticking like a wooden clock?
Will she go slimy like the trail of a snail?
Start singing like a humpback whale?
Will she go *roar* like an army truck?
Start quacking like a fluffy duck?
Who knows? Not I. Let's wait and see.
(I'm glad it's neither you nor me).
Oh, Grandma, if only you knew,
What I have got in store for you!

Edith Drysdale (8)
Walmley Junior School, Sutton Coldfield

My Friend, My Very Own

Oh, what joy it is to have a friend like you,
You taught me how to play games the way you do,
Our friendship is a thick wall,
That will never ever fall,
You are my stunning star that I caught falling from the sky,
I held you in my palm and raised you up high,
You are my Cupid who opened my eyes and shot my heart,
Superglued it so it never came apart,
Oh, what joy it is to have a friend like you,
You taught me how to play games the way you do,
You looked into my eyes,
And heard my cries,
And supported me through,
Like a true friend should do.

Anneisea Thoto Cameron (10)
Walmley Junior School, Sutton Coldfield

My Lively Life

I have a pet mouse,
He lives in my penthouse,
It costs billions of pounds,
As big as five football grounds.

My car, a Lamborghini SUV,
Is parked right next to the sea,
Next is my private plane, which looks insane,
Like my other train dancing in the rain.

Just to mention, I'm a fighter pilot,
And I ride in a freezing cold climate.

Because I'm a billionaire,
I'm famous everywhere,
But just cos I'm a billionaire,
Don't try to rob me -
Or you will be *sorry!*

Veer Bhalla (10)
Walmley Junior School, Sutton Coldfield

My Favourite Animal

Some cute little whiskers
And a bright pink nose
Do they whisper?
No one knows!

How quick they run,
Full of grace
With lots of fun
In an open savannah space.

With black spots hidden under the golden fur
They walk with a gentle purr,
And pounce on scared antelopes
That have got no hope!

I wonder if you ever run out of breath
What do you do, take a rest?
Can you guess my animal?
Look below to see if you're correct.

Answer: A cheetah.

Tabitha Abraham (8)
Walmley Junior School, Sutton Coldfield

My Teacher

My teacher's name is Miss Pearson
Not so fearsome, I'd like to say...
In fact, my teacher is very kind
And likes to read in her mind.
My teacher encourages me to do my best
And often puts me to the test.

My teacher is funny and happy
And hardly gets snappy,
She's simply the best
And stands out from the rest.

For all the things you have taught me,
I know I can be a little bit naughty
But I can't thank you enough for being you
My teacher, Miss Pearson.

Raine Dee (8)
Walmley Junior School, Sutton Coldfield

A Tropical Holiday

Sipping from a coconut on a hot, sunny day,
I dip my toes in the calm sea bay,
The waves wash over the golden sand,
And sun shines on this tropical land,
With pretty flowers sparkling in the sun,
Building sandcastles, having so much fun,
But now, my time here has come to an end,
I wish I could stay with my newfound friends,
I board the plane so we can fly sky-high,
And soon realise that this is not goodbye!

Till we meet again!

Daisy Bray (9)
Walmley Junior School, Sutton Coldfield

The Pirates' Poem

There was a pirate called Fred
Who didn't get out of his red bed.
There was a pirate called Sue
Who never got out of the loo.
There was a pirate called Jill
Who fell down the hill.
There was a pirate called Pete
Who had smelly feet.
There was a pirate called Penny
Who had lots of pennies.
There was a pirate called Claire
Who always went to the funfair.
There was a pirate called Ben
Who made a big den.

Erynn Jacks (8)
Walmley Junior School, Sutton Coldfield

Birds

What is it that you see in the sky?
Next to the clouds? Let me have a guess,
Is it a plane nearby,
Flying in its happiness?

What has feathers that are so soft,
Or talons like a dagger,
Carelessly held aloft?
Perhaps a bat with eyes that are shinier,
Than a glowstick in the dark.

What has two eyes and a beak?
Good question, what is it?
I have the answer, let me speak,
It is a bird (I admit)!

Amy Kong (9)
Walmley Junior School, Sutton Coldfield

Queens Of The BFFs!

Me and my friends blend in with each other
Being funny and spreading the glee
We go to the park but, before, we snore
As we go on the swings, we sing our favourite song!
When we get lost, we cry out loud
I look up high in the sky
The bright blue tells me the true love of friendship
Eye to eye, I see them multiply
We hug each other until we go home
And now we all know that we are the queens of
Friendship!

Gianna Antonia Jeevan (11)
Walmley Junior School, Sutton Coldfield

Unflinching

U nder pressure for your amusement
N ever get distracted!
F ocus on your video entertainment
L eave the game if someone is bullying you
"I might win or I may lose!"
N o cheating!
C ourageous control wins the game
H appy and fearless make you stay brave.
"I nspire your idol!"
N o being disrespectful
G aming is challenging.

Rehan Afzal (9)
Walmley Junior School, Sutton Coldfield

Feelings Of Nature

N ature is a very beautiful, satisfying place.
A ll the pretty plants and colourful trees are there to be enjoyed.
T ry to stop and listen for the peaceful sound of the birds
U p high in the bright blue cloudy sky.
R esting on the mossy green grass, I feel relaxed as the cool breeze gently blows against my arms and knees.
E verybody should go outside and experience the beauty of nature.

Oliver Mushing (8)
Walmley Junior School, Sutton Coldfield

Amidst The Moon

You shine in the night like a magical light,
Going through different phases each day and night.
For you are the moon,
As pretty as can be,
That shines amongst the myriad of stars.
When days seem as if they'll never end,
You rise up when the day is done.
You shimmer like smoke as you reflect onto the water,
Always looking so close,
When in reality,
You're so far.

Maisy Coombs (11)
Walmley Junior School, Sutton Coldfield

Nature

Nature, you are so beautiful with your blossom trees and your buzzing bees.
The grass is green and the water is so clean.
What could be more great than lying in the sun with your mate?
But we are not kind to it as there is plastic everywhere we sit.
There is so much pollution in the air, does anyone seem to really care?
We all need to come together as one to help the planet we live on.

Imogen Holliday (9)
Walmley Junior School, Sutton Coldfield

Books Are Everywhere

Books, books and even more books.
Books are everywhere.
One day,
Mother even had one in her very own hair

Books are great.
Books have meanings
A thing I know is,
Books give you all sorts of feelings.

Anyone can read books,
Anywhere and everywhere.
But one thing you have to do is,
Read them with care.

Daya Chana (10)
Walmley Junior School, Sutton Coldfield

Weasels!

I like weasels,
They are long and brown.
When I don't get to see them,
It makes me frown.

They live in the snow,
And eat mice.
They also eat squirrels,
And think they are nice.

They do not hibernate,
Just like bears do.
They love to play in the snow,
Just like me and you!

Lily Miller (11)
Walmley Junior School, Sutton Coldfield

Summer

S ummer is from June to August.
U nderneath the dancing sun that smiles down on us
M any people across the world enjoy summer
M aybe fool and play around with an ice cream
E veryone should enjoy summertime and BBQs
R oasting sun high in the sky whilst we play and have fun.

Reggie Butler (9)
Walmley Junior School, Sutton Coldfield

My Love

M adie, who loves being an investigator!
Y ou love sweets!

L ove is important as well as help!
O nly share time and love, it will make a difference!
V ery little time and love from you will not make a difference
E vie is Madie's mum and she is a sweet worker.

Gracelyn Noby (8)
Walmley Junior School, Sutton Coldfield

Beach Party

B eautiful beach
E xtraordinary sights
A bsolutely amazing
C rashing waves
H ave fun

P iggyback on the beach
A mazing ice cream, no
R eading on the beach, go
T o the beach
Y es, let's go to the beach!

Leah Sangster (9)
Walmley Junior School, Sutton Coldfield

Poppy Day

R emember, remember in this month of November
E veryone who survived.
M ost of all
E veryone who died.
M ourn over lost ones.
B ut you see
E veryone we lost
R eally just wanted us to be free...

Zaynab Deen (9)
Walmley Junior School, Sutton Coldfield

My Trip To The Safari Park

I love going to the safari park and feeding the animals there.
The rhinos, giraffes, lions and tigers, but there is no bear.

After seeing the animals, we go on some fair rides. Then we might pop into the shop.

We had an awesome day out.

Mia-Rose Burbidge (8)
Walmley Junior School, Sutton Coldfield

Enchanted Forest

Enchanted forest, where can you be?
Might you be left, might you be right? I see
A foxy Doxi.
Might I ask you, foxy Doxi
Where can the enchanted forest be?
Can you be in the clouds,
Can you be hidden in the ground
Where can you be?

Elise Lee Allen (9)
Walmley Junior School, Sutton Coldfield

Animal Kingdom

Dogs are funny
Cats are fluffy
Lions are feisty
Monkeys are funky
Birds are fast
Ducks are fat
Bears are furious
Tigers are frightening
Sheep are fuzzy
Fish are fishy
Bees are friendly.

Alex Husak (8)
Walmley Junior School, Sutton Coldfield

People

People, oh people
Different shapes,
Different noses,
Different names,
Different hair and
Different colours.
We are all different.

Ayla Noor Bajwa (7)
Walmley Junior School, Sutton Coldfield

The Successful Future

I have always dreamt of being a pilot since I was about five years old
I am very anxious to be a pilot
I cannot wait because whenever an aeroplane flies in the sky,
I always wish to be on the plane.
Also, when I was coming to the United Kingdom,
As we were at the checkpoint, our pilot passed by, so I had the opportunity to see the pilot rushing toward departure of AT554 flight
I was very anxious to get on the plane so I could know how they fly
As we boarded, I felt comfortable and wished I was in the cockpit to fly the plane.
The taking off was scary, I had never entered a plane!
What an unforgettable experience.

Erijesu Adeniran (10)
Westcott Primary School, Hull

My Magical Future!

My future is to be a make-up artist,
To own a salon,
To do make-up, nails, hair, perfume, fake nails and more glam
And help people, help the homeless, help as many people as I can.

To have three dogs, three cats and six rabbits
Dogs: Lilac, Taravi and Tyia,
Cats: Blossom, Lulu and Meadow.
Rabbits: Riley, Lily, Daisy, Molly, Maisie and Libby.

I want to live in Australia with my friends
And look at animals.

I want to be a mum of two kids, twin girls and maybe even two more boys
Don't have to be twins.
Girls: Lunar, Skylar.
Boys: Dylan and Leo.
And a fiance, girl or boy.

Phoebe McCoid (10)
Westcott Primary School, Hull

Flying All Across The World

When I grow up, I want to be a flight attendant,
Flying all over the world,
It's a dream,
Flying to Turkey, flying to Spain
Or I could take a train,

A private plane would be nice,
Or a private room on a train,
As long as I get to Turkey or Spain,
I would take my three kids on a plane

I would love to fly to Hawaii, but it would be a pain,
Flying would be better to take a plane to Hawaii than a train,
Taking three kids on a plane is my dream
Arriving after all the flying would be great
Trying all of Hawaii's fresh fruit.

Eva Brewin (10)
Westcott Primary School, Hull

The Actor Of My Dreams

If scared, I scream
If sad, I cry
If happy, I'm excited
If worried, I'm scared
Eyes of the world shining,
Like stars as I perform in front of my kingdom's stage
Standing, my heart beating very, and I mean very, fast.
As I clap, other people clap and when I act, they clap more.
I have to try, try, try to get better, better, better
I can do it
It frightens me when I act like a scaredy-cat
As I wait for my turn for my part, I freak, freak out.
The world is watching me and so are you.

Lily Procter (10)
Westcott Primary School, Hull

Save The Animals

Sitting, worried
Saving innocent little creatures from terrible fates.
From a small helpless kitten to a scaly big Komodo dragon.
Power of healing and helping distressed animals.
Fish, birds and even flowers are living things, and help them.
All sorts of animals.
Taking pulses left and right
Like a high-technology robot multitasking.
Checking for viruses and sickness with a shot of my powerful, ice-cold needle
I stick into their skin.
Removing raging bacteria like an ant-eater.

Savannah Booker (9)
Westcott Primary School, Hull

Wonderful Actress

I stand on that stage, the lights shine on me
I wear a red dress that is as red as my heart,
I act, I am being fantastic,
The lights shine to the end of the moon,
I will be amazing with this,
I am proud like I've won a reward,
Hoping I will get this job,
So I can make people shine in the dark,
That means people will be a star to me,
I have always wanted to be an actress, so
I can make people feel proud of themselves,

My dreams and my hopes fill with new hope.

Evie Wharam (9)
Westcott Primary School, Hull

Nursing Beliefs

Being a nurse is the world to me,
I'll be able to help people with,
Life-saving treatment,
I'll work harder to put a smile on their faces,
Help people be joyful and happier in life.

If there was a short-lingering bang,
I would be the first person to see what it was,
And if it was a patient, I would,
Give the patient the care they needed.

The world would rely on me,
They would rely on me to do the work,
And they would believe in me.

Mia Hampshire (10)
Westcott Primary School, Hull

The Dream Of Passion

Here I am,
I am my art,
As I follow my dream,
Watching my art displayed in an art gallery,

Squeak, screech, squeal,
When they see me, I turn as bright as the sun
Thinking that my job is done,
But then I look into my kingdom.

I know my passion isn't over yet,
Because, still, my art dances with children come near,
Love yourself and do what's best,
Because no one can judge,
If you are just simply you.

Elise Hampshire (10)
Westcott Primary School, Hull

Teacher

To help people care,
To help get better and just get the education they need,
I don't need to give up,
It is my dream come true for life.
I'm relieved to be on stage,
To help the planet so it is singing,
With children that can go to school.
Why don't people like school?
I make it fun so kids would like to come to school.
For my life and dream to come true,
I would be so much happier and joyful.
I'm so hopeful,
It can be beautiful.

Isabelle Kirby (9)
Westcott Primary School, Hull

Dream To Achieve

Police are here,
Drop everything out of your hands,
Or stay calm,
When police are here.

Police are here,
Pull over,
Or just relax and breathe,
We will give you the phenomenal freedom we've got,
Safety is key,
When police are here.

Everyone relying on me like a queen,
Catching criminals like no one before me,
It's our time to shine like stars,
Your safety is key,
When police are here.

Neve Symons (9)
Westcott Primary School, Hull

My Creative Future

My dream is to be an artist,
I love to do art whatever it may be
Drawing, painting is my dream.
Drawing is creative
And fascinating for many people, including me.
Watercolours, pastels
And much more, all the colour inspires me to
Draw and it should for you too!
With art, you can do
Many things, maybe
You could colour
Things like a playground set of swings?
I love to draw
And to do much more!

Gracie Reid (10)
Westcott Primary School, Hull

My Future Hopes And Dreams

I will fight for peace and joy.
I'm as bright as the fire in my heart.
I'm as kind as the cold winter sky when the
Moonlight pours down.
Standing here as the sky and sea kneel before me.
I'm as sweet as sugar and everything nice.
I'm as royal as a king.
I'm as smart as time.
I shimmer like amethyst,
Time to shine,
Time to shimmer,
Time to fight.

This is me...

Emily Underwood (10)
Westcott Primary School, Hull

My Hopes And Dreams

My dream is to be an artist and to care for animals
All around the globe, no matter the type
They all need love and care
Travel around the globe to draw landmarks
Australia, New Zealand, South Africa and more
I hear splashing of the paint
Splash, squeak, splash
A hope of a Zizer Ginger to name it Nutmeg
To be with friends
To live the most
And for my hopes and dreams.

Ebony Barker (10)
Westcott Primary School, Hull

My Animal-Tastic Dream

Zookeeper is my dream,
To help poorly animals
And to breed the animal theme
To get dogs called Rosie, Leo and Westly

I would also like to move to Australia,
To see the Great Barrier Reef,
The kangaroos are trampolines,
The sand is the Earth.

Zebras, tigers, pandas, koalas are the animals I want to work with,
Animals, animals are my thing,
I will now put some music on to sing.

Jessica Atkin (10)
Westcott Primary School, Hull

My Football Future

Me, a footballer, gliding across the pitch,
The ball a rocket flying towards the goal,
Gradually flies faster and faster and it hits the post,
Crash, bang, thud,

The next Messi rises,
The glory, the fans,
Time to shoot, time to score,
We will win the World Cup,

Suarez falls,
The GOAT rises,
The next Messi,
Train, fight another war that begins.

Charlie Davison (10)
Westcott Primary School, Hull

My Dream

The tunnel's doors open,
Light flooding in,
The green kingdom awakens,
I stand there, between two soldiers,

The whistle blows,
Like a rocket blasting off to space,
The ball is fired towards,
Them... The beautiful sound,
Of the ball smacking against the post,
Vibrates around the world,
The whole world watching,
The crowd like wild animals,
Playing for ultimate glory.

Ellis Hall (10)
Westcott Primary School, Hull

Actress Believes In You

Eyes of the world,
Shining like stars,
As I perform,
My kingdom is my stage.

Earn lots of money,
Work on the script until the show,
We will never give up,
Try our best.

Standing here, in front of a crowd,
Keep trying,
To show how good we are.

Waiting for the claps,
To do different movies and shows,
Believe in yourself and remember all of your lines.

Phoebe Fletcher (9)
Westcott Primary School, Hull

The Future Me

I am the one who is the saviour of the world,
I save people like a superhero,
I am going to try and make everyone safe.

Who stops people's crimes?
I do,
I chase the horrible people
Who make crimes, as fast as a cheetah,
The only thing I want
Is to get rid of crimes.

I will always try to get people happy,
I will always make everyone
Have a better life.

Marjan Khaksar (10)
Westcott Primary School, Hull

My Future Self

Standing here as proud as an emperor
Working out the Y and X
Standing here at the front of the class
Am I the best teacher ever?

Silly, super, science
Magic, methodical, maths
What's the answer to this?
All hands shoot up

I'm a walking dictionary.
"Miss, how do I spell this?"
Time for French
What is better, writing or RE?

Jessica Todd (10)
Westcott Primary School, Hull

My Dog Dream

My dogs could sniff for my success
Dogs faster than a flash,
No pup too small, no pup too big,
Dogs will be my friends.

Dogs will give me a treat in life,
The puppies are like a blanket,
Hope to become big in the world,
Born and ready to do this and always will be,
Lick with their tongues, giving love,
Time to begin
Time for success
Time to help.

Layla Carr (9)
Westcott Primary School, Hull

My Future

I'm standing at the front
Every shining star is facing me
Let's learn about me
I would love a puppy, Cookie,
I would earn lots of money and a big house
All the pupils looking at me
Let's do maths
All hands shoot up
I'm a walking dictionary
I'm the teacher with the answer
I want to be inspirational
And now the class is silent.

Mila Fleming (10)
Westcott Primary School, Hull

My Wonderful Show Just For You

Standing here, in front of a crowd
Waiting for claps to show how good we are
Keep trying
To do different movies and shows
To show how good we are
Believe in yourself and remember your lines
Earn lots of money
Work on the script till the show
We never give up
Try our best
Eyes of the world
Shining as I
Perform on my kingdom stage.

Evie Sellers (9)
Westcott Primary School, Hull

My Lovely Dreams!

My hopes and dreams
Many of my dreams are not
There... But these are my dreams, I wish
I'll be a model
Model, all I wish I will be, I'll be a model
But I want to have two kids
Girl and a boy
Girl name: Anna
Boy name: Davies
And those are my dreams
I wish they will be true,
But there's more to see
In *life!*

Maria Ciuperca (10)
Westcott Primary School, Hull

My Hope And Dream

I want to fix cars such as
Lambos, Ferraris,
Mustangs, McLarens,
Bugattis, and any car.

When I'm older, I
Would like a blue motorcycle,
The cars are rusty,
Old and fast.

When I'm older, I
Will get paid lots
Of money,
If I want
To fix cars, I will
Have to go under
Them.

Noah Sanderson (10)
Westcott Primary School, Hull

Dance-Off

As you step, you think
You are you, think you're
Going to fail.
Just try your best
Just beat the rest
The dazzling uniform, reflection of the stage
Lights shimmer everyone
Working hard, me
Just trying to help.
The music stops
Everyone is heavy breathing
Holding hands in the
Air, bowing.

Elsie Mae Cassells Robinson (9)
Westcott Primary School, Hull

The Future Me

Saving, saving,
Like no one has,
Don't give up,
Try, try, try,
Don't let anyone score again,

No more goals from them,
We are successful,
Once again,
The crowd rise from the ashes,
They know that his saves are not over yet,
Oh... Ooh...
He saves the last kick of the game.

Joey Dale (10)
Westcott Primary School, Hull

Unknown

Capture criminals,
Then interrogate them,
They try to run,
They get tased,
They try, try, try again,
Bzzzzz,

I make YouTube shorts,
Or, or, or YouTube videos,
Then make lots of lots of money,
Then buy, buy, *aaah*,
Rainbow Lambo and *aaah*,
Mega mansion.

Alfie Cawkell (10)
Westcott Primary School, Hull

Me In The Future

This is my chance,
And maybe my only chance,
To show the world who I am,

The world inspires me
Art is me
And it is my time to show the world

My art dances in the sunlight
Ready to be seen

It is time to inspire
Time to paint
Time to throw
Time to be me.

Olivia Hickson (10)
Westcott Primary School, Hull

The Future Me!

Try, try, try again
Don't give up,
It's now or never,

Don't get distracted
Just focus,
Don't be pressurised,
Just try

Be a champion,
Be a master,
Be the best,
Don't give up,
Bang, bang, clap.

Jasmine Thompson (10)
Westcott Primary School, Hull

Footballer

Scoring and scoring over again,
And, after another and another
He was more than successful, he was golden.
It was as if he rose from the ashes,
Again. Before he knew it, he was off
To Wembley and he loved hearing the crowd
Erupting from the ashes.

Deacon Russell (10)
Westcott Primary School, Hull

My Train Life

Work hard to achieve,
Achievement I have made,
Don't feel pressured,
Chug, chug, chug,
The train going as fast as a cheetah,
Carries passengers to their destination,
We have made it,
Our journey is over.

Oliver Anderson (10)
Westcott Primary School, Hull

Python

P atiently waiting for its prey
Y oung hatchlings being protected
T op of the food chain
H iding deadly venom
O utstandingly fast
N ever go near a python.

James Cooper (10)
Westcott Primary School, Hull

My Success

Achievement you want to make
A change you want to make
As you walk down the road of success
But never look back to failure
Don't feel pressured
Keep calm.

Oliver Priest (9)
Westcott Primary School, Hull

Turtle

T op of the food chain
U nder the sea
R oams so beautifully
T errific
L ovely, royalty of the seas
E xtremely adorable.

Archie W (9)
Westcott Primary School, Hull

YOUNG WRITERS INFORMATION

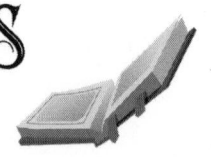

We hope you have enjoyed reading this book – and that you will continue to in the coming years.

If you're the parent or family member of an enthusiastic poet or story writer, do visit our website **www.youngwriters.co.uk/subscribe** and sign up to receive news, competitions, writing challenges and tips, activities and much, much more! There's lots to keep budding writers motivated!

If you would like to order further copies of this book, or any of our other titles, then please give us a call or order via your online account.

Young Writers
Remus House
Coltsfoot Drive
Peterborough
PE2 9BF
(01733) 890066
info@youngwriters.co.uk

YoungWritersUK
YoungWritersCW **youngwriterscw**

Scan me to watch the Poetry Towers video!